MW00939569

THIRTY DAYS IN COLOSSAE

A DEVOTIONAL COMMENTARY ON PAUL'S LETTER TO THE COLOSSIANS

GARY BLACKARD

Rebekah
May you be blessed in
all your work as you serve
our Lord. Thank you for all
you have done for ATC.
Better Together
in Christ
Gary Bl[illegible]

WESTBOW
PRESS®
A DIVISION OF THOMAS NELSON
& ZONDERVAN

WestBow Press books may be ordered through booksellers or by contacting:

WestBow Press
A Division of Thomas Nelson & Zondervan
1663 Liberty Drive
Bloomington, IN 47403
www.westbowpress.com
1 (866) 928-1240

ISBN: 978-1-9736-8916-4 (sc)
ISBN: 978-1-9736-8917-1 (hc)
ISBN: 978-1-9736-8915-7 (e)

Library of Congress Control Number: 2020906149

Print information available on the last page.

WestBow Press rev. date: 07/01/2020

Dedication

This devotional commentary is dedicated to the women and men of Adult & Teen Challenge in the United States and around the world. May the Lord continue to transform lives through his power and saving grace.

I'd also like to dedicate this work to my parents, Bill and Faith Blackard. They raised my sister and me in the Word and have shown us what true living in Christ really is.

A special thank you to Dr. Dan Morrison, navy chaplain and professor at the Assemblies of God Theological Seminary at Evangel University. Dr. Morrison edited and gave good counsel.

All proceeds from this book will go to Adult & Teen Challenge.

How to Use This Commentary

Everyone has personal preferences when reading and studying the Bible. Below are tips and recommendations to use this commentary effectively. Start somewhere and remain consistent in studying God's word.

1. Open all reading times with a simple prayer. Ask the Lord to reveal his word to you. Ask him for clarity and insights. God will answer this prayer.
2. Read the passage(s) of scripture. All scripture from Colossians comes from the English Standard Version (ESV) of the Bible. You can read in different ways: silently, aloud, at a normal cadence, or slowly.
3. Once you have read the scripture selection, read the commentary found following the selected passages.
4. This commentary references passages outside of Colossians. As you encounter them, read them, especially referenced verses given. The reference will provide additional insight regarding the text of Colossians. It will also provide examples of how scriptures relate to each other. Further, it will ensure context is kept while reading and studying.

5. As you finish reading, end your time with a brief prayer. Ask the Lord to help you apply the scripture to your life. Ask the Lord to bring the verses to mind throughout your day.

May the Lord fill you with understanding and with wisdom as you seek him through his Word. May the Holy Spirit embolden you and encourage you to live out the Word.

CONTENTS

Finding Your Identity and Function in Christ

Paul, an apostle of Christ Jesus by the will of God, and Timothy our brother, to the saints and faithful brothers in Christ at Colossae: Grace to you and peace from God our Father.[1]

Paul's role as an apostle of Christ Jesus reveals that Jesus called him to serve in this way according to the will of God. He understands that God initiated his call and placed him in the body of Christ to function as he does.

Even more important than his function, Paul recognizes his identity in relation to Christ, Timothy, and the Colossians. He addresses the church at Colossae in religious and relational terms. He calls them "saints and faithful brothers." He recognizes the members of the church at Colossae as those who have been declared holy in Christ. Rooted in that relationship with Christ, Paul recognizes himself, Timothy, and the Colossians as members of God's family.

Sometimes Christians do not recognize their identity in Christ or their function in his body. At other times, some despise their function because they do not like how God has called them to serve. Others become arrogant, comparing their function to others. No

---

[1] Colossians 1:1–2.

matter the temptation one experiences regarding his or her function in the body of Christ, God sees everyone equally. Every person who follows him is his child. His grace fills people's hearts, giving a peace that they cannot fully understand. This is a peace that guards hearts and minds, protecting each person from the stresses of a world filled with anxiety.

Ask God how he wants you to function in the body of Christ and truly come to understand what it means to be his child. May God continue to extend his grace and peace to those he calls his children.

Reflection Questions

As a believer, are you quick to align yourself with Christ even when you are amid those who do not believe in him or follow him?

Do you understand what it means that God called you and brought conviction and compassion to your heart and mind?

When you read scripture, who do you understand yourself to be?

How has God called you to function in the body of Christ?

Giving Thanks

We always thank God, the Father of our Lord Jesus Christ, when we pray for you, since we heard of your faith in Christ Jesus and of the love that you have for all the saints, because of the hope laid up for you in heaven. Of this you have heard before in the word of the truth, the gospel, which has come to you, as indeed in the whole world it is bearing fruit and increasing—as it also does among you, since the day you heard it and understood the grace of God in truth, just as you learned it from Epaphras our beloved fellow servant. He is a faithful minister of Christ on your behalf and has made known to us your love in the Spirit.[2]

Paul and the other believers with him thanked God while praying for those in the church at Colossae. They brought the church's needs to God, knowing that he takes care of his children. They prayed for strength, peace, blessing, and conviction. Their prayers reflect the faith they had in Christ and result from the love the Christians at Colossae had for their fellow believers.

The church at Colossae loved the saints, worked hard to support them, and wanted nothing but the best for them. Why? They received the gospel and understood the power it gave in the hope of

---

[2] Colossians 1:3–8.

eternity. This realization drove the behaviors of strengthening faith and loving one another.

Thankfulness is not easy when enduring tough times. It is not easy when the bank account is empty. It is hard when there is no food. Circumstances do not diminish the blessings that people have and the need to give thanks for them. While many people cannot see things to be thankful for, others wish for the blessings and benefits that some take for granted.

Remember to give thanks in every season of life and trust God with every situation.

Reflection Questions

How often do you pray for the church and for others?

What situations in your life make it difficult for you to give thanks to God?

For what in your life can you give thanks to God?

Walking in a Worthy Manner

And so, from the day we heard, we have not ceased to pray for you, asking that you may be filled with the knowledge of his will in all spiritual wisdom and understanding, so as to walk in a manner worthy of the Lord, fully pleasing to him: bearing fruit in every good work and increasing in the knowledge of God; being strengthened with all power, according to his glorious might, for all endurance and patience with joy; giving thanks to the Father, who has qualified you to share in the inheritance of the saints in light.[3]

Since Paul and his companions heard of the love the Colossians expressed, they consistently prayed for them, asking the Lord to fill them with the knowledge of his will, wisdom, and understanding. This was so they might "walk in a manner worthy of the Lord." This kind of walk is pleasing to God. It results in fruit, strength, and thanksgiving to God.

Those who follow Christ must walk in a manner that is worthy of the Lord—a manner pleasing to him. Every Christian should want to live God's glory and purposes. This happens through having relationships that honor God and through doing actions that align

[3] Colossians 1:9–12.

with scripture. This means doing *everything*—work, hobbies, and all other activities—as for the Lord. Reading his Word and praying, enjoying his creation, and using the talents and skills he has given (naturally and through education) please him. Aim to grow in these areas, giving glory to him.

In accord with Paul's prayer for the Colossians, increase in the knowledge of God. This can only be done by spending time in his word. Through the Word, learn what pleases God and confidently walk in a manner that the Lord would deem worthy.

Reflection Questions

What aspects of your life do you believe are not pleasing to God and do not reflect walking in a manner worthy of the Lord?

What aspects of your life do you believe are pleasing to God and reflect walking in a manner worthy of the Lord?

What can you do to help ensure that your life and actions are pleasing to the Lord?

NEW CITIZENSHIP

[God the Father] has delivered us from the domain of darkness and transferred us to the kingdom of his beloved Son, in whom we have redemption, the forgiveness of sins.[4]

God has chosen those in Christ as his inheritance—as his children of light. The blood of Jesus Christ qualified those who have this status. There are no other ways to qualify. The death and resurrection of Christ sealed this hope in him. When people accept Christ as Lord and believe in his deity, they are transferred from the domain of darkness into the kingdom of Christ. This is a change in citizenship. Moving from the kingdom of darkness into the kingdom of Christ highlights the transfer from being an enemy of God to being a son of God and a coheir with Christ.

In Christ's kingdom there is redemption and the forgiveness of sins. This truth is often mind-blowing. Jesus, out of his great love for humanity, came and lived among humans, as a human, without sinning so that he could be the perfect sacrifice for the sins of humanity. In his death, there is redemption. In his resurrection, there is life eternal. He gives his children eternity in a new heaven and a new earth where they will enjoy his presence. Heaven is more than clouds and a harp. Heaven is more than singing at the feet

[4] Colossians 1:13–14.

of Jesus for one hundred thousand years. It is the cleanest water flowing in streams, rivers, and lakes. It is the ability to interact with wildlife without worry or fear. The colors will be more brilliant, and the food will taste amazing! Jesus, the Redeemer, made the way for all to experience this new citizenship. He wants all to taste and see that he is good.

Live each day recognizing that while we are citizens of an earthly kingdom for now, citizenship in God's kingdom takes precedence over all.

Reflection Questions

Having been delivered from the domain of darkness, what aspects of your current life reflect your former life outside of Christ?

How does your citizenship in heaven impact how you live?

Who do you have in your life to help you in living out your new citizenship in God's kingdom?

In Christ All Things

He is the image of the invisible God, the firstborn of all creation. For by him all things were created, in heaven and on earth, visible and invisible, whether thrones or dominions or rulers or authorities—all things were created through him and for him. And he is before all things, and in him all things hold together.[5]

Christ is the image of God, the firstborn of all creation. This does not mean that Christ was created; he is eternal. Christ is God; he is *the* image of the invisible God. When the heavens were made, Christ was there. All things were created by Christ, through Christ, and for Christ. He reigns supreme and will continue to do so in eternity.

Jesus Christ is eternal and the creator of all things. He is before all things, and in him all things hold together. He is in control of it all. People may never understand this side of heaven (there are many things in this life we will not understand), but they must understand that Christ is the supreme ruler of all things. Nothing surprises him. Nothing catches God by surprise. The exponential growth of technology, including artificial intelligence and mixed realities, does not make the Lord wonder. He knows all. He gave all. He is all. What a hope for all who put their trust in him.

---

[5] Colossians 1:15–17.

Those things in life that appear to be broken, even the things that are broken, can be placed into the hands of the one who holds all things together. When he holds them together, they cannot remain broken, for in him all things hold together.

Reflection Questions

What in your life has caught you by surprise?

What is happening that makes it feel as if your life is falling apart?

What is causing you negative stress in life that you wish would simply go away?

Leading in Reconciliation

And he is the head of the body, the church. He is the beginning, the firstborn from the dead, that in everything he might be preeminent. For in him all the fullness of God was pleased to dwell, and through him to reconcile to himself all things, whether on earth or in heaven, making peace by the blood of his cross.[6]

Jesus is the head of the church. His sacrifice on the cross and his resurrection have made the way for all to have eternal life. He is the hope of the world. Life is filled with joy, with sorrow, with laughter, and with pain. Through it all, Jesus surpasses everything.

In Christ all the fullness of God was pleased to dwell. This is what makes his grace so powerful. Jesus Christ is God. The fullness of God—God the Father, God the Son, and God the Holy Spirit—rests in him. Christ can provide for all, no matter the situation: the disease, the financial despair, or the emotional pain. Christ is the Lord who provides.

Christ supplies reconciliation. The love of God drew him to reconcile people to himself. Christ, in his fullness, became the reconciliation for all things, earthly and heavenly, and that through

---

[6] Colossians 1:18–20.

his blood shed on the cross, the peace that passes all understanding flows in the hearts of his children. Praise belongs to Christ alone for his unfailing love and sacrifice in making the way for everyone to be reconciled to God.

God gives to those who follow him the ministry of reconciliation. This requires of all who follow Jesus to make sure that amid their reconciliation with God that they also experience reconciliation with others. Make your relationship right with God by making right your relationship with others.

Reflection Questions

Is Christ preeminent in your life?

Does Christ's righteousness lead your decisions, your actions, and your thoughts?

With whom do you need to be reconciled?

Stable and Steadfast

And you, who once were alienated and hostile in mind, doing evil deeds, he has now reconciled in his body of flesh by his death, in order to present you holy and blameless and above reproach before him, if indeed you continue in the faith, stable and steadfast, not shifting from the hope of the gospel that you heard, which has been proclaimed in all creation under heaven, and of which I, Paul, became a minister.[7]

Every human being was born as a sinner. Through the fall of Adam, sin became human nature. Everyone was alienated from God because of sin. In society, people consistently make rebellious statements about God, and millions accept them as the norm. Christians need to pray for those who are alienated from God, while standing firm for biblical principles through compassion and love. Instead of being Christlike and showing compassion and love, Christians can get too caught up in spewing hateful words toward others.

Humanity's alienation from God has been resolved by the reconciliation of Christ's death and resurrection. Christ's work enables those who become children of God to live holy and blameless lives—lives above reproach—before Christ. Christ has completely

---

[7] Colossians 1:21–23.

removed the guilt and shame of sin for eternity. Because of the blood of Jesus Christ, those who are in Christ are unblemished in the eyes of God. Admittedly, Christians still commit sin while here on earth, but even that sin has been cleansed through his grace. When the judgment occurs, the sins Christians have committed will not be found, as they are buried with Christ. Christ will present his church as holy and blameless, as the church continues in the faith, remaining stable and steadfast.

Reflection Questions

What sin have you committed lately?

How do you feel about the fact that Christ presents you as holy and blameless before God even though you have committed sin?

Suffering for the Sake of Others

Now I rejoice in my sufferings for your sake, and in my flesh I am filling up what is lacking in Christ's afflictions for the sake of his body, that is, the church, of which I became a minister according to the stewardship from God that was given to me for you, to make the word of God fully known, the mystery hidden for ages and generations but now revealed to his saints. To them God chose to make known how great among the Gentiles are the riches of the glory of this mystery, which is Christ in you, the hope of glory.[8]

Christ said that Christians would suffer for his cause. Therefore, Christians should rejoice amid their suffering, as they are enduring such hardship for Christ's sake. Paul suffered much, but he explained that it was not to be compared with the future glory to be experienced. The story of Paul's conversion shows that Christ can change the heart of any man or woman, no matter how much he or she has done. Paul considers his stewardship as a called minister of the gospel. He knew his call was to expound the word to Gentiles. We are all called to make the word of God more fully known, through our actions and through sharing testimonies of what God has done for us.

---

[8] Colossians 1:24–27.

God's love and presence have been revealed to all. Contemplating and reflecting on the grace, mercy, and love of Christ highlights the greatness of the mystery that has now been revealed to those who follow him. God chose to make known to his saints—his children—the very mystery, which is the hope of Christ, who dwells in every believer. God is in, with, and among his people.

Let the revelation of this mystery guide you in how you live and how you treat those with whom you interact.

Reflection Questions

Do you feel that you have ever been mistreated because you are following Christ? If so, how?

Have you ever mistreated someone because he or she was following Christ?

How do you pray for people who are suffering for the name of Jesus Christ?

Him We Proclaim

Him we proclaim, warning everyone and teaching everyone with all wisdom, that we may present everyone mature in Christ. For this I toil, struggling with all his energy that he powerfully works within me.[9]

Paul knew the value of his calling. He had to proclaim and teach everyone who would listen about the love of Christ. He also had to warn them of the dangers of not responding positively to God's love. He went beyond this initial teaching to focus on maturity in Christ. He encouraged people's ability to teach others how to grow in their faith and live strong, healthy lives in the faith by which they were saved.

Christians are called to grow in Christ and proclaim the message of the gospel to others. Paul noted the hard work of sharing the gospel, but he recognized from where the real power came. Christ powerfully works within those who are open to God using them. All of Christ's followers have this assurance. Christ works in each one as everyone grows in his grace and righteousness. He will use individuals to impact and influence others. For example, an act as simple as publicly praying over your meal and giving thanks in a

---

[9] Colossians 1:28–29.

restaurant can have a positive impact on the restaurant staff and other patrons. Christians can proclaim Christ in a variety of ways.

Ask God to provide opportunities to proclaim him in ways that will have a positive impact on the world.

Reflection Questions

Is your faith growing?

How deeply do you feel you know the word of God?

Do you have compassion for the lost?

For whom do you pray on a regular basis?

Transformation Through Relationship

For I want you to know how great a struggle I have for you and for those at Laodicea and for all who have not seen me face to face, that their hearts may be encouraged, being knit together in love, to reach all the riches of full assurance of understanding and the knowledge of God's mystery, which is Christ.[10]

Paul was filled with love for the church of Christ. He struggled with the fact that he could not be present with some of them. He wanted to spend quality time in their presence, sharing the glory of Christ. He struggled with the lack of personal interaction. He wanted to see for himself how these believers were encouraged in the faith and how they engaged in relationship with one another. There are depths to understanding all the blessings and gifts from God. Many Christians live on the surface of God's love and never fully immerse themselves in the pleasures and riches of scripture and other spiritual disciplines. Not because they must but because they desire to.

The deeper one gets in the understanding and knowledge of God through Christ, the fuller life becomes. God designed things this way. Christ came, died, and rose again so those who put their trust in him can live full lives. Jesus's work enables humanity's redemption from sin and people's transformation into a new creation.

Accepting Christ as Lord and Savior is only the beginning of a transformed life. Growth occurs through sanctification by

---

[10] Colossians 2:1–2.

Christ building people's character, shaping their thoughts, and strengthening their faith. This is not an easy process, but it is filled with hope, peace, and encouragement. Allow your heart to be encouraged today, as Paul hoped for the Colossians so long ago.

Reflection Questions

Who in your life has God used to bring about transformation and growth?

Who do you encourage to transform and grow in Christ?

Treasures of Wisdom and Knowledge

In [Christ] are hidden all the treasures of wisdom and knowledge. I say this in order that no one may delude you with plausible arguments. For though I am absent in body, yet I am with you in spirit, rejoicing to see your good order and the firmness of your faith in Christ.[11]

The Old Testament prophet Isaiah wrote of how God said Christ would have the Spirit of wisdom and understanding, of counsel, of might, of knowledge, and of the fear of the Lord. King Solomon tells us that the fear of the Lord is the beginning of wisdom. Why? Because all wisdom begins with God, who through his Son Christ and the work of his Holy Spirit builds up the knowledge and wisdom of humanity and brings treasures along with it.

Consider the women and men in history who were considered very wise, and the gifts they gave the world: inventions, economic vitality models, forms of better government, activism, and equality for all. These are just some of the treasures wisdom and knowledge have brought, but none could come without the hand of God in them. He is the source of all wisdom. There are depths of wisdom,

---

[11] Colossians 2:3–5.

love, peace, and joy that we must always strive for. In Christ, they are never-ending.

Ask God to grant wisdom and knowledge that more treasures may be shared with the world, and he many receive glory.

Reflection Questions

How have you tapped into the source of wisdom and knowledge?

How much do you rely on Christ for wisdom and knowledge?

How often do you ask God to move your mind and heart to be centered on him?

Walking in Christ

Therefore, as you received Christ Jesus the Lord, so walk in him, rooted and built up in him and established in the faith, just as you were taught, abounding in thanksgiving.[12]

People who acknowledge Jesus Christ as their Lord and Savior accept a mandate to walk in Christ. What does this mean? The church must learn to walk in Christ, following his traits, his character, and modeling his actions. Paul told the church at Ephesus to walk in three ways: walk in love, walk as children of light, and walk wisely. This is how all Christians should be walking in Christ. Christians must show his love to everyone around them. They should engage in and with their communities, living real lives in front of real people, not hiding away or staying within their silos. Each person needs to be a light to those who are walking in darkness. Christian lives must reflect the light of Christ. In this way, Christians walk in love, in their position as God's children, and in wisdom.

Without roots, plants and trees die. In many plants, the taproot is one of the most important. It finds the source of water quickly and helps to stabilize the plant. Therefore, Christians must be rooted in Christ. He supplies believers with the life-giving nourishment that can only come from him. Those who follow Jesus should be filled

---

[12] Colossians 2:6–7.

with appreciation and joy, abounding in knowing Christ rose again and provides them access to the endless supply of abundant life they have in him.

The best expression of thanksgiving anyone can provide for the life Christ has given is to walk in him, reflecting that life to those in the world around him or her.

Reflection Questions

How are you walking in love?

How are you walking as a child of the light?

How are you walking in wisdom?

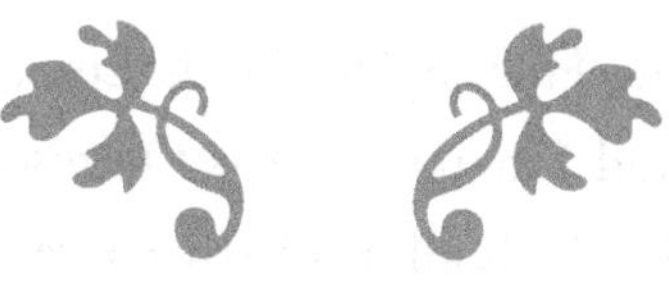

FILLED WITH CHRIST

See to it that no one takes you captive by philosophy and empty deceit, according to human tradition, according to the elemental spirits of the world, and not according to Christ. For in him the whole fullness of deity dwells bodily, and you have been filled in him, who is the head of all rule and authority.[13]

The Colossians had been exposed to much false teaching claiming a higher knowledge that was not from Christ. Paul refers to this false teaching as empty deceit. It was nothing more than worthless deception. Today, the broader society and the many in the church have fallen into false teaching. The world today accepts the teaching of many religions rooted in deception and attempt to draw people away from the person and work of Jesus Christ.

This verse is not saying that Christians should avoid philosophy or science. Paul is putting the proverbial stake in the ground by stating that any philosophy that does not align with Christ is worthless and deceitful. All of science aligns with Christ because he is the Creator of the universe. Wisdom and knowledge begin with him. If people recognize that, Christ will continue to reveal his creation and his power through the gift of science.

Paul delivers the foundational principle that in Christ the

13 Colossians 2:8–10.

fullness of deity dwells. Christ has all the attributes of God the Father and God the Holy Spirit. He is Love, Peace, Joy, Grace, Mercy, Wisdom, and Strength. He is Omniscient, Omnipresent, and Omnipotent. Christ is all in all. Therefore any philosophy that does not align with Christ is worthless.

Paul reminds the church that they have been filled with Christ, who is the head and rule of all authority. Christ is the head of all. He is authority defined.

Reflection Questions

How do you submit to the authority of Christ in your life?

What do you see in the broader society that challenges the authority of Christ?

How have you undermined the authority of Christ in your life?

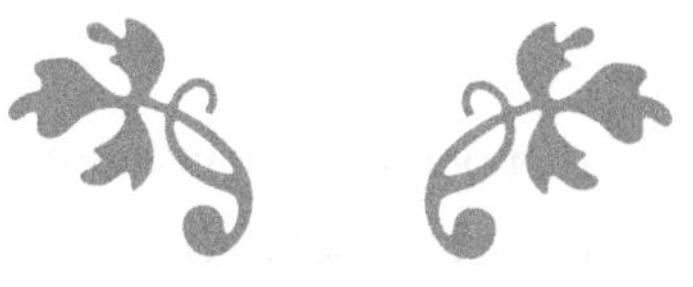

Buried and Raised with Christ

In [Christ] also you were circumcised with a circumcision made without hands, by putting off the body of the flesh, by the circumcision of Christ, having been buried with him in baptism, in which you were also raised with him through faith in the powerful working of God, who raised him from the dead. And you, who were dead in your trespasses and the uncircumcision of your flesh, God made alive together with him, having forgiven us all our trespasses, by canceling the record of debt that stood against us with its legal demands. This he set aside, nailing it to the cross. He disarmed the rulers and authorities and put them to open shame, by triumphing over them in him.[14]

Paul speaks of the circumcision made without hands, referring to the spiritual circumcision where sin is removed from a believer, and new life is given. The old flesh being put to death when Christ died on the cross, and those who follow Jesus are raised in him through his resurrection. He is Redeemer and Rescuer. Through Christ, *all* our sins are forgiven. What a powerful promise. Greed, envy, lust, gluttony, anger, pride, and hate are all washed in the blood

---

[14] Colossians 2:11–15.

of Christ. Those who are in Christ now live in and with Christ, protected by him.

The record of debt that people have because of their sins has been canceled. This means that those who follow Jesus are no longer to the law of death. They no longer must pay for their sin with death because the debt has already been paid. How? That sin was nailed to the cross through the hands and feet of Jesus Christ. The death and resurrection of Christ disarmed the rulers and authorities—Satan and the spiritual authorities that sought to destroy humanity through sin. Satan has no authority over the children of Christ; he is powerless against us. The triumph of Jesus Christ has given us eternal life in him. Therefore, give thanks for the eternal effects of the burial and resurrection of Jesus Christ.

Reflection Questions

Though you have been buried and raised with Christ, what struggles do you currently experience in your walk with God?

From what has Jesus redeemed and rescued you?

The Substance Belongs to Christ

Therefore let no one pass judgment on you in questions of food and drink, or with regard to a festival or a new moon or a Sabbath. These are a shadow of the things to come, but the substance belongs to Christ.[15]

The church at Colossae experienced judgment from many in the Jewish population regarding their lack of participation in dietary practices, festivals (the annual religious celebrations or feasts such as Passover, Pentecost, and/or Tabernacles), the new moon (the monthly sacrifice), and the Sabbaths. The false teachers passed judgment on these Christians, but Paul told them to not get caught up in it. Christ came to earth, died, and rose again. He is the substance of all things that were celebrated and acknowledged in the food regulations and the feasts. He is to be celebrated as the Messiah who has come.

Jesus said that the Sabbath was made for man, not man for the Sabbath. The idea was rest. Humans were made to rest in the Lord from time to time (weekly is still a great discipline). This time of rest does not mean that people must stay on their knees and meditate for twelve hours. People can experience rest in God by the means of a long walk in nature, reading a good book, prayer time, relationship

[15] Colossians 2:16–17.

building, and eating in community. Of course, this assumes people are already spending quality time with Christ. Spiritual disciplines such as reading the Bible, prayer, fasting, solitude, simplicity, and service belong in the lives of all Christians. The more time spent with Christ, the more those who spend time with him grow to be like him.

Set aside time for him. Rest in him. Celebrate the Sabbath.

Reflection Questions

How will you rest in God today and this week?

What spiritual disciple(s) will you practice in the coming weeks?

Which spiritual discipline do you find the most difficult?

Nourished in Christ

Let no one disqualify you, insisting on asceticism and worship of angels, going on in detail about visions, puffed up without reason by his sensuous mind, and not holding fast to the Head, from whom the whole body, nourished and knit together through its joints and ligaments, grows with a growth that is from God.[16]

The apostle Paul addressed serious issues occurring in the church at the time he wrote the letter to the Colossians. Those issues still occur in many areas of the church today. Jewish leaders and mystic teachers tried to influence the church by insisting on asceticism and the worship of angels, paying special attention to visions driven by sensuality and emotions. These false teachers practiced this self-denial to show themselves worthy, humbled before God. This form of humility was really pride in in their own works.

Paul told the Ephesians that they are saved through faith by the grace of God and not of their own works. A person's works cannot result in salvation or holiness. Only Christ can do this. Now this does not mean there is not a place for works. The Bible is very clear that God will reward each person according to his or her works. These works cannot be the focus or the "why." They serve as the "how" of the Christian's focus, which is Christ. If a person focuses

[16] Colossians 2:18–19.

on Jesus, these works become natural activities that are done because that person is a follower of Jesus.

Unlike Paul, these false teachers were not holding fast to Jesus Christ, the Head. If believers are firmly connected to Christ, they will see spiritual growth and will be nourished by the love, peace, strength, and wisdom of God found in him who died and rose again.

Reflection Questions

In what ways have you tried to show others that you were worthy and humbled before God?

Why do you do the works you do?

Self-Made Religion

If with Christ you died to the elemental spirits of the world, why, as if you were still alive in the world, do you submit to regulations—"Do not handle, Do not taste, Do not touch" (referring to things that all perish as they are used)—according to human precepts and teachings? These have indeed an appearance of wisdom in promoting self-made religion and asceticism and severity to the body, but they are of no value in stopping the indulgence of the flesh.[17]

If people have been found dead and risen with Christ, why would they continue to follow vain things, which prove to have no value? Rules and regulations filled the hearts of some of the people in Colossae, and deep legalism spread across the church. This is still an issue today in many churches and denominations. In some denominations, dancing, women wearing makeup, women in pants in church, men without ties in church, and secular music were forbidden and considered sinful. Paul found this type of ascetic teaching in Colossae, and he aimed to correct the church regarding their practices.

These types of rules and regulations have an appearance of wisdom in promoting religion, but they are of no value in stopping the indulgence of the flesh. The work of humans cannot solve sin-filled

[17] Colossians 2:20–23.

nature of humanity. Only the work of Christ can do this. Therefore, Christians must give their fleshly desires to Jesus and allow the Lord to work through them. This is the process of sanctification. Christ enters the lives of those who invite him and begins to develop their character to be like him. This is both a joyous and painful process but one everyone goes through as they journey with Jesus.

Walk the road of transformation and avoid the dangers of self-made religion.

Reflection Questions

Have you ever found yourself struggling with a sin and wondering how you will ever get rid of it? If so, what sin?

What rules have you seen/heard that you think are a form of self-made religion?

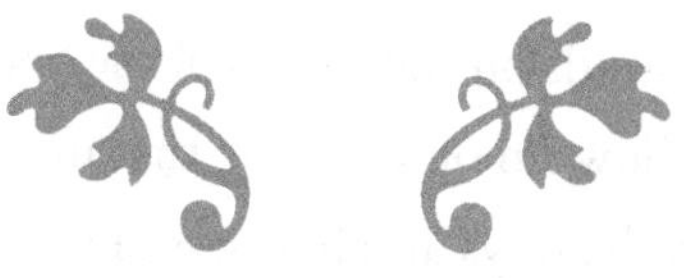

Raised with Christ

If then you have been raised with Christ, seek the things that are above, where Christ is, seated at the right hand of God. Set your minds on things that are above, not on things that are on earth.[18]

Since Christians have been raised in Christ, they are to focus on the attributes and character of God in heaven, where Christ is seated with him. Our minds should be filled with the things of heaven. An adage says do not be so heavenly minded that you are of no earthly good. While the intent of this statement is good (focus on work for Christ here on earth), it is misleading. For Christians, their hearts and minds should be intensely focused on the things of God. In doing so, they should be much more effective here on earth. Christians have a call to seek first the kingdom of God and his righteousness; then all these things will be added to you. What are the "things" to be added? They are the areas of life that people think about such as food and clothing—the basic needs in life. These items are critical to survival, yet Jesus calls those who follow him to seek him first. The same thing applies in this passage.

Sin abounds in this world, and the human mind needs protection. An element of this protection is the ability to think on things above—on Christ and his ways. Those who live according to

[18] Colossians 3:1–2.

the flesh set their minds on the flesh, and those who live according to the Spirit set their minds on the things of the Spirit. This is a critical principle. Do not allow sin or anything that may be unfruitful or in direct conflict with the ways and holiness of God to enter the mind. Remain focused on Christ.

Reflection Questions

What do you normally think about throughout your day?

In what ways do you believe setting your mind on things above will help you be more effective in ministering to others?

What things in the world serve as a distraction to you seeking God's kingdom first?

Hidden with Christ

For you have died, and your life is hidden with Christ in God. When Christ who is your life appears, then you also will appear with him in glory.[19]

The old self has died. A new creation has come. This is what occurs when Christ enters the heart and transforms the person from the inside out. To be hidden with Christ in God means eternal protection as believers. No man or woman, not even Satan himself, can remove someone from the hand of Christ. The life of the believer is intertwined with Christ, who is forever intertwined with God. While the world may not see Christ, he is ever present with those who put their trust in him. Believers understand that Christ is omnipresent. Therefore, they are never alone as children of God.

The Christian life must be centered on Christ so much so that there is a recognition that without Christ, life lacks significance. Pray for God's wisdom and grace to enter in and take hold. Believers should recognize Christ as the source for everything. He has the living water that he offers freely to all who are thirsty and need a drink. Such water brings refreshing in times of dryness, despair, and comfort. May Christ fill the heart to overflowing, providing peace—incomprehensible peace—amid the various seasons of life.

---

[19] Colossians 3:3–4.

Reflection Questions

Does everything center on Jesus? If not, why not?

In what ways does your life not center on Jesus?

DEAD OR ALIVE

Put to death therefore what is earthly in you: sexual immorality, impurity, passion, evil desire, and covetousness, which is idolatry. On account of these the wrath of God is coming. In these you too once walked, when you were living in them. But now you must put them all away: anger, wrath, malice, slander, and obscene talk from your mouth. Do not lie to one another, seeing that you have put off the old self with its practices and have put on the new self, which is being renewed in knowledge after the image of its creator.[20]

Those who are in Christ have been raised with Christ. They are no longer bound to sin even though their "flesh" is drawn to it. Not only are they no longer bound, but they should put their sinful nature aside. Paul lists several elements of sin including sexual immorality, impurity (we know what is pure and not pure according to Christ), passion, evil desire, and covetousness, a form of idolatry. This list is ever-present in society, and many believers are caught up in the web of sin's deceit. Many justify what appears on television or social media believing it will not harm their thinking or spiritual lives. Many are trapped in the materialism of this world, justifying their hearts without realizing their real intent. This is what Paul was warning the Colossian church about.

---

[20] Colossians 3:5–10.

Christ has transformed his people, and they should live in holiness and the blessing of the purity that comes under the power of Christ's sacrifice. For God's wrath comes for the sin-filled disobedient people. There will come a day, a judgment day, when all will be held accountable for their sin. Christians will be rewarded for their lives lived for God.

Live each day remembering that those who are dead to sin are alive in Christ and should remember to live as those who have experienced new life in him.

Reflection Questions

Does your life promote sin such as malice?

Does your life give way to crude thinking and jokes? Do you allow your eyes or ears to see and hear such communication?

Do any of these sins rule over you? How is your communication with others? Is it filthy, angry?

IDENTIFYING OTHERS

Here there is not Greek and Jew, circumcised and uncircumcised, barbarian, Scythian, slave, free; but Christ is all, and in all.[21]

Far too often, societies try to divide people based on race, ethnicity, social class, economic status, and any other way that one can find a way to highlight division. When it comes to the church, Paul explains that these divisions do not matter. Why? Because Christ is all and in all. He is the one who unifies in every sense of the word.

It seems reasonable that Jews and Gentiles would not get along. Animosity between those of different social classes would seem realistic. Though siblings can sometimes have rivalries, those who are in Christ should recognize themselves as children of God and brothers and sisters in the faith. Christ sees the race, ethnicity, social class, economic status, and every other distinction that people use to bring about division. Instead of highlighting division, these distinctions reflect the beauty of the diversity within God's creation and the potential benefits of what can happen when brothers and sisters come together in unity.

Instead of using the distinctions between people to bring about division, explore the benefits of joining with different people to help further the kingdom of God in the world.

---

[21] Colossians 3:11.

Reflection Questions

How do you treat those who have a different social, racial, or economic status than you?

In what ways can people who are not like you help you grow as a follower of Jesus?

Bear with One Another

Put on then, as God's chosen ones, holy and beloved, compassionate hearts, kindness, humility, meekness, and patience, bearing with one another and, if one has a complaint against another, forgiving each other; as the Lord has forgiven you, so you also must forgive.[22]

Rules followed by men and women will never make them holy. The Holy Spirit does the work of sanctification in the people of God. However, the work of sanctification still requires a willingness to obey. Temptations and trials will come, but those who follow Christ have received a call to put sin to death in their bodies. This is what real living is all about. No matter the circumstance, the illness, the financial stress, or the hurt from others, dependence on God's provision as his beloved will be all people ever need. All people are dear to the heart of God. He loves his creation to unimaginable depths. God loves people even when they fall, fail, or hurt. Therefore, rest in God's love today.

God calls his children to have compassionate hearts and be filled with kindness, humility, meekness, and patience. People are designed for relationships. Humans are social beings created by a social God. God wants people to interact with him and with one another. If they are missing from life, people should pray for them to

[22] Colossians 3:12–13.

be evidenced in their lives. The Colossians received the instruction to bear with each other. This instruction applies to all who follow Jesus. When complaints arise, forgive one another. Why? Because God has forgiven all who follow Christ. The children of God must care for one another with authenticity and grace. This is not a request, but a command.

Reflection Questions

Is your heart compassionate toward God? Toward others?

Are you patient? If not, why not?

What does it mean to be the beloved of Christ?

PEACE AND LOVE

And above all these put on love, which binds everything together in perfect harmony. And let the peace of Christ rule in your hearts, to which indeed you were called in one body. And be thankful.[23]

Considering yesterday's reading, which can be difficult, the Bible provides guidance for how to do the seemingly difficult things it calls for. Successfully bearing with one another requires putting on love. Christians should first be filled with love above all these other attributes. Why? Because love binds everything and everyone together in perfect harmony. Love should be the basis of everything because God is love. Christ gave his life out of love. As a result, he has called and commanded all who follow him to love. He calls them to love one another and to love their enemies.

The peace of Christ should rule in hearts of those who follow him. Peace begins and ends with Christ. This magnificent peace comes from knowing that the God of the universe, through his son Jesus Christ, loves everyone, died for everyone, and rose again for everyone!

The peace that comes from Christ does not fade away. Cancer and other diseases cannot take this away. Bankruptcy or financial

---

[23] Colossians 3:14–15.

ruin cannot take this away. Broken relationships, divorce, and death cannot take this away. This calls for celebration! His love and peace alone should fill hearts and minds with joy and thanksgiving. Consider all the Lord has done, and give thanks.

Reflection Questions

How thankful are you?

Do you celebrate thanksgiving to God regularly?

For what have you not been thankful?

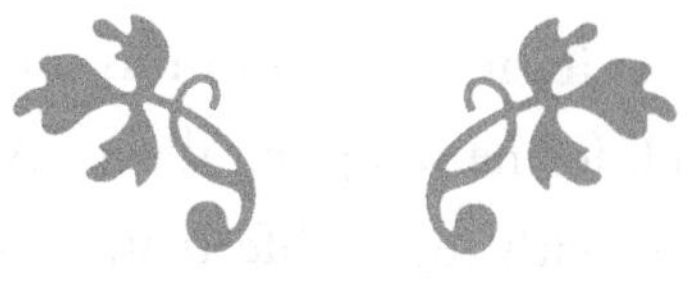

In Jesus's Name

Let the word of Christ dwell in you richly, teaching and admonishing one another in all wisdom, singing psalms and hymns and spiritual songs, with thankfulness in your hearts to God. And whatever you do, in word or deed, do everything in the name of the Lord Jesus, giving thanks to God the Father through him.[24]

When the word of Christ dwells in those who believe, it should affect how they live. God's people are to live holy lives, filled with the love and goodness of Christ. Knowing how God's word has called people to live, accept the challenge of scripture and aim for that which seems impossible, allowing Christ to perform his work by the power of the Holy Spirit. Part of living holy lives means teaching others the doctrines, the commands, and the love of Christ so that each one can help others grow in his love. People were created for relationship, first with God and then with one another. Those who follow Jesus need each other to help lift up, to encourage, to point out wrongdoing, to love deeply, and to pray for various needs.

Considering how God calls his people to live, they should do everything in the name of the Lord Jesus Christ. This can be extremely difficult. Humans fail from time to time. However, this should not be an excuse for not trying. Christians are to surrender

[24] Colossians 3:16–17.

their words and deeds to Christ and become more like him. This is the process of sanctification. And in this process, people are to be thankful to God, for he has given them new life—a life more abundant and filled with joy. A life that, even during times of suffering, has a peace that passes all understanding. For this, always give thanks.

Reflection Questions

Is the word of Christ at home in your life?

How does your speech reflect the name of Christ?

How do your actions align with the word of Christ?

All in the Family

Wives, submit to your husbands, as is fitting in the Lord. Husbands, love your wives, and do not be harsh with them. Children, obey your parents in everything, for this pleases the Lord. Fathers, do not provoke your children, lest they become discouraged.[25]

Paul says a lot about family relationships. He tells wives to submit to their husbands. He calls on husbands to love their wives and highlights the kind treatment the man should show toward the woman he loves. Paul moves on to the relationship between parents and children, calling children to obey their parents and fathers not to provoke their children.

Children raised in obedience to parents, whom they can see will, be more open to being obedient to God, whom they cannot see. The obedience to parents also comes with a blessing—the first command in the Bible to do so.

This obedience does not mean obeying parents over God's laws. Unfortunately, many parents today live ungodly lives and pressure their children to do the same. A teenager accepting Christ as his or her Savior could be disobeying an atheistic parent but has every right in God's eyes to do so.

Fathers (and mothers) should not provoke their children. Fathers

---

[25] Colossians 3:18–21.

should expect obedience but out of love, not out of only direct fear. In the days of Paul's writings, fathers could be abusive, and the rights of children and women were not considered. Paul was challenging this approach and saying that fathers should love and encourage their families.

All of these are forms of love and submission. Find ways to show love and submission to those in your family.

Reflection Questions

Growing up, in what ways did your family of origin reflect Paul's instructions regarding familial relationships?

In what ways did your family not reflect Paul's instructions?

What struggles do you presently have with the instructions found here in scripture?

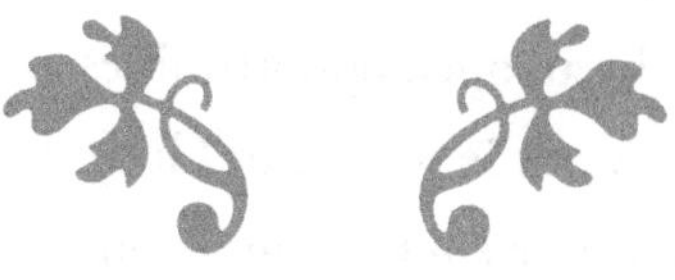

SERVING THE LORD

Bondservants, obey in everything those who are your earthly masters, not by way of eye-service, as people-pleasers, but with sincerity of heart, fearing the Lord. Whatever you do, work heartily, as for the Lord and not for men, knowing that from the Lord you will receive the inheritance as your reward. You are serving the Lord Christ. For the wrongdoer will be paid back for the wrong he has done, and there is no partiality. Masters, treat your bondservants justly and fairly, knowing that you also have a Master in heaven.[26]

God created humanity to work. He designed humans to be active in the kingdom of God doing a variety of tasks. When God placed Adam in the garden, he told Adam to dress it and keep it. Prior to humanity's fall into sin, Adam maintained the garden. Even after sin entered the world, the call to work remained. Work became harder as a result of sin. Despite the difficulty, work was originally created for and remains for the benefit of God's creation.

Work for the believer is worship to God. Every moral and good task done well is a way to worship God. Work should glorify God.

Work should contribute to others. God intended work to bring pleasure, not only to those doing it but to other individuals and to broader communities. Work affects peers, leaders, those who follow,

[26] Colossians 3:22—4:1.

and those who are served, including the family that benefits from the work done. Work can open opportunities for conversations with others to share how work is service to God. If not done well, poor work can serve as a negative reflection on one's Christian testimony.

No matter one's place in society, do all work as service to God and treat others fairly. For God shows no partiality.

Reflection Questions

How do you worship God through your work?

What impact do you believe your work can have on others?

How do you treat those for whom you work or supervise? Does your behavior reflect Christ to them?

Steadfast Prayer

Continue steadfastly in prayer, being watchful in it with thanksgiving. At the same time, pray also for us, that God may open to us a door for the word, to declare the mystery of Christ, on account of which I am in prison—that I may make it clear, which is how I ought to speak.[27]

Paul calls on the Colossians to "continue steadfastly in prayer." He asks for prayer for himself and his team so they can preach the word with clarity and effectiveness. He wants to be able to share the mystery of Christ and his salvation for all humanity, doing so as best as possible.

Fellowship with Christ begins with daily prayer. Just as relationships with family members and friends require consistent communication, so does a relationship with Jesus. Growing in him requires consistent communion with him. Prayer is critical to both the spiritual and physical life. Jesus told his disciples to pray. The prayer life of the church should consist of both listening to God's voice and sharing needs and requests with him. Such a prayer life should also be filled with thanksgiving and praise to God.

God has saved his people from sin, has justified them, and continues to sanctify them until they join him in eternity—an

[27] Colossians 4:2–4.

eternity filled with unimaginable joy and fellowship. Jesus has done so much for each one. Every person owes his or her health, joy, love, and abilities to the Maker of all things. He loved humanity enough to die for all. He wants each person to grow in the knowledge of him so he can perfect them for his glory.

Pray Paul's prayer request to one another. May the Lord teach his people to speak his word effectively and to proclaim the news of the gospel with boldness and clarity.

Reflection Questions

How often do you pray?

Do you listen for God's response during your prayer times?

In what ways do you believe God has answered your prayers?

Seasoned with Salt

Walk in wisdom toward outsiders, making the best use of the time. Let your speech always be gracious, seasoned with salt, so that you may know how you ought to answer each person.[28]

Christians have received a call to treat outsiders (unbelievers) with respect without getting caught up in their ways (sin). Paul tells the Colossians to be wise in all they do—including interacting with those who do not believe in Christ—doing so in love. Everyone's speech should be "seasoned with salt." Salt preserves. Salt deters corruption. In the same way that salt can do these things, a person's speech, seasoned with salt, should bring preservation and should deter corruption in the lives of those with whom they interact.

Every person deserves to be loved and respected, even those considered the worst of sinners. This is the dichotomy of true Christianity. Christians are to hate the sin and evil but love the person who commits the sin. The time is short. Therefore, make the best use of the time, as good stewards. God has graciously given life, and he expects people to use their time on earth wisely.

The words spoken to others should be filled with grace. A believer's righteousness, through the cleansing power of Christ, should be used to help bring cleanliness to all around them. Be ready

[28] Colossians 4:5–6.

for such testimony opportunities. While not all are called to preach, all are called to testify and witness to what God has done for them.

Pray for opportunities, and ask the Lord to give boldness, wisdom, and readiness. Pray for words seasoned with salt with the hope of helping preserve one's life and helping all to avoid corruption.

Reflection Questions

When is the last time you witnessed to someone about the love of Christ in your life?

How can your words be seasoned with salt?

With whom to you plan to have your words seasoned with salt?

Are you ready to give others the answers to why you are different—changed, transformed?

Encouragement and Comfort

Tychicus will tell you all about my activities. He is a beloved brother and faithful minister and fellow servant in the Lord. I have sent him to you for this very purpose, that you may know how we are and that he may encourage your hearts, and with him Onesimus, our faithful and beloved brother, who is one of you. They will tell you of everything that has taken place here.

Aristarchus my fellow prisoner greets you, and Mark the cousin of Barnabas (concerning whom you have received instructions—if he comes to you, welcome him), and Jesus who is called Justus. These are the only men of the circumcision among my fellow workers for the kingdom of God, and they have been a comfort to me.[29]

Paul closes the letter to the church at Colossae by acknowledging those who are ministering with him and on his behalf. He mentions Tychicus, Onesimus, Aristarchus, Mark, and Justus (also called Jesus). Tychicus and Onesimus were sent to the Colossian church to tell them of the activities of Paul and others while also to minister on behalf of Paul to encourage the Colossians.

While Paul mentions Tychicus and Onesimus encouraging the

---

[29] Colossians 4:7–11.

Colossians, he explains that Aristarchus, Mark, and Justus fulfill another function. These men were fellow servants who served as a comfort to Paul. They were all part of the same body, but they served distinct functions.

Paul's words highlight how people should surround themselves with great friends who care about them, will comfort them, and will encourage them. This should also remind Christians to ask God how he wants them to function in the body as an agent of comfort or encouragement in the lives of those around them. May all discover who God wants them to comfort or encourage each day.

Reflection Questions

Do you have friends in your life that provide you with encouragement and comfort?

Are you an encourager? How often do you encourage others?

Do you acknowledge those who work with you?

PASS THE WORD

Epaphras, who is one of you, a servant of Christ Jesus, greets you, always struggling on your behalf in his prayers, that you may stand mature and fully assured in all the will of God. For I bear him witness that he has worked hard for you and for those in Laodicea and in Hierapolis. Luke the beloved physician greets you, as does Demas. Give my greetings to the brothers at Laodicea, and to Nympha and the church in her house. And when this letter has been read among you, have it also read in the church of the Laodiceans; and see that you also read the letter from Laodicea. And say to Archippus, "See that you fulfill the ministry that you have received in the Lord." I, Paul, write this greeting with my own hand. Remember my chains. Grace be with you.[30]

Epaphras served the Lord and consistently prayed for the church in Colossae. His prayers included prayers for spiritual maturity and full assurance in the knowledge of God the Father and Jesus Christ. Paul witnessed the hard work of Epaphras on behalf of the Colossians and those in Laodicea and Hierapolis.

Paul made it clear to have his letter read to others while also asking that his letter to the Laodiceans be read by the Christians at Colossae. Paul also directs one of the ministers at Colossae,

[30] Colossians 4:12–18.

Archippus, to fulfill his ministerial duties faithfully, as given by the Lord.

God has given each person gifts and talents. Like Epaphras and Archippus, all followers of Jesus have a responsibility to use their gifts and talents seriously and invest them in the kingdom of God, expecting returns for Christ. God calls all Christians to share the message of Jesus with others. Luke, who was a physician, contributed to the spread of the message by traveling with Paul and writing the Gospel of Luke and the book of Acts. Follow God's guidance in passing the word of Christ to others.

Reflection Questions

What are some of the gifts and talents you have received from the Lord?

How do you plan to use your gifts and talents for the sake of other people?

Day Thirty

Today, we want you to pause and take a moment to reflect on the last month. What has God been saying to you through Paul's letter to the Colossians? Follow the simple process below:

1. Block 45 minutes today
2. Get your Bible, a journal or notepad, a pen/pencil and your favorite beverage
3. Pray now for God to reveal his word to you
4. Take some time to read the entire book of Colossians again. Read all four chapters in one sitting
5. Pause and think on what you have read
6. Underline phrases or words in the letter that stand out to you
7. Journal/write your thoughts out answering the questions what is this scripture telling me and how can I practice living it out in my life?
8. Show/discuss with someone you trust as a Christ-follower/friend
9. Apply the learnings, one at a time
10. Celebrate when you have seen results or differences in your life

About the Author

Gary Blackard is president and CEO of Adult & Teen Challenge USA, which is a biblically-based nonprofit focused on alcohol and substance abuse recovery. Prior to his current role, he served in executive roles at Evangel University and Xerox Corporation. As a pastor, he sees the transformative power of the word of God in everyday life. He is married to his high school sweetheart, Debbie, and has two married children and four grandchildren. He lives in Ozark, Missouri.